MONET

Monet

BY YVON TAILLANDIER

CROWN PUBLISHERS, INC. - NEW YORK

Title page: EDOUARD MANET
MONET'S FLOATING STUDIO (Detail), 1874
Oil on canvas, 32¼″ × 39⅜″ (82 × 100 cm)
Bayerische Staatsgalerie, Munich

Series published under the direction of:
MADELEINE LEDIVELEC-GLOECKNER

Illustrations and layout:
MARIE-HÉLÈNE AGÜEROS

Library of Congress Cataloging in Publication Data

Taillandier, Yvon.
    Monet.

    (Crown art library)
    1. Monet, Claude, 1840-1926 — Criticism and
interpretation.   I. Title.
ND553.M7T313 1982   759.4   85-13247
    ISBN 0-517-08885-1

PRINTED IN ITALY – INDUSTRIE GRAFICHE CATTANEO S.P.A., BERGAMO
© 1987 BONFINI PRESS CORPORATION, NAEFELS, SWITZERLAND
REVISED EDITION

TERRACE AT SAINTE-ADRESSE, 1867. Oil on canvas, 38⅝″ × 51⅛″ (98.1 × 129.9 cm)
The Metropolitan Museum of Art, New York

The year is 1874.   There are sounds of waves, of oars in the water, and of leaves rustling. The Seine near Argenteuil is hidden by the low-hanging branches of a row of trees. Sunlight strikes the jacket of a stroller, tracing patterns upon his shoulder.   With a quick gesture he pushes the branches aside.   Slowly, a boat moves off from the bank of the river.   A bearded man in his thirties, stoutish and short, is at the oars; he is dressed in a white smock and wears a bell-shaped hat.   This is not a fisherman about to cast his line into the stream, nor an oarsman with a passion for rowing, but an artist

Tree Trunks, 1857. Sketchbook.   Black lead, 11¹³⁄₁₆″ × 9″ (30 × 23 cm)
Musée Eugène Boudin, Honfleur

6

on his way to paint from nature. He has taken his boat out today and may have decided to paint the Seine from a point out in the stream. The stroller on the bank recognized him at once, although few people in 1874 would have known much about the man in a white smock, a landscape artist with a preference for painting water. Nevertheless, an exhibition of paintings, etchings, and sculpture at the studio of the photographer Nadar, 35 Boulevard des Capucines, in Paris, featured a canvas of his, hung among those of his artist friends with a similar taste in art. The painting was called *Impression: Sunrise* (see page 32), and it prompted a journalist to coin a neologism which was to become famous. The word "sunrise" now seems full of symbolic meaning, but at the time it conveyed nothing to the journalist. He retained only the word "impression" and later invented

Man Sitting Under a Tree, 1857
Sketchbook. Black crayon, 11″ × 7⅞″ (28 × 20 cm)
Formerly in the collection of
Michel Monet, Giverny

"Impressionists." This word, however, was meant to be derogatory, and those to whom it was applied were usually thought of as mad. The man out strolling near Argenteuil has sound reasons for not sharing this opinion. But for the moment, this is not what is on his mind. He is laying down a heavy box on the grassy bank and a wooden contraption which he had been carrying across his shoulder. Then, standing upright again, he shades his eyes from the fierce summer sun and looks at the boat: It is a small boat with a little cabin, deck space, and a mast. When Claude Monet, the man in the white smock, later spoke of his modest vessel, he described it as a barge.

Monet has been called "The Raphael of Water" and "The Inventor of Color." He was also a painter of light, and he may have been the first artist to capture "the moment in time" and depict the most fleeting aspect of nature. His work could also be viewed as a starting point for the Neo-Impressionists, the intimist Nabis, and later the Cubists, Abstractionists, Abstract Expressionists, as well as contemporary artists inspired by calligraphy and minimalism. He stimulated the first reactions that followed

River Bank, 1856.   Black crayon, 15⁵⁄₁₆″ × 11³⁄₈″ (39 × 29 cm)
Musée Marmottan, Paris. Bequest of Michel Monet

FLOWERING GARDEN, ca 1866.   Oil on canvas, 25⅝″ × 21¼″ (65 × 54 cm)
Musée d'Orsay, Paris

THE PICNIC LUNCH (Left Panel), 1865-1866
Oil on canvas
164⁹⁄₁₆″ × 59¹⁄₁₆″ (418 × 150 cm)
Musée d'Orsay, Paris

◁

▷

THE PICNIC LUNCH (Central Panel), 1865-1866
Oil on canvas
97⅝″ × 59¹⁄₁₆″ (248 × 150 cm)
Musée d'Orsay, Paris

WOMEN IN THE GARDEN, 1866-1867.   Oil on canvas, 100¾″ × 81⅞″ (256 × 208 cm)
Musée d'Orsay, Paris

Impressionism, leading to Neo-Impressionism and abstract art. In 1880, a solo exhibition of Monet's work in the gallery La Vie Moderne served as a turning point for the Pointillist Paul Signac. And it was Monet's *Haystacks* that so struck Wassily Kandinsky, first at an exhibition of French Impressionists in Moscow in 1895, and later at the Munich Secession show in 1900. Kandinsky was irritated at first by the fact that the painting was so imprecise that he had to look in the catalogue to see what it was supposed to be. Soon, however, his annoyance was swept away by the brilliance of the colors. He was overwhelmed by a splendor created entirely by color and had his first intuition that the object is not an indispensable element in a painting. Monet also heralded a nowadays widespread interest in Eastern art. Finally, his depiction of space, compositions, and creative technique can be very modern. However, in spite of the fact that he could be regarded, with Paul Cézanne, as the father of modernism, he is more often called "The Father of Impressionism."

Monet was not the oldest of the Impressionists: Camille Pissarro, born in the West Indies in 1830, was ten years older. He did not always exhibit with the Impressionists: They held eight exhibitions between 1874 and 1886; Pissarro took part in all eight, while Monet abstained from the fifth, sixth, and eighth show. Pissarro was so constant a member of the group that he could write that his life coincided with the history of Impressionism. Monet justified his absence from several exhibitions on the grounds that the group did not keep to its initial program and therefore he viewed Pissarro's faithful participation in the group as a breach of faith in the theories originally espoused by the Impressionists. He felt that he alone of the group had remained untainted and uncompromising. This steadfast attitude helped the Impressionists to stay the course and comforted them throughout the great difficulties they encountered for most of their career, for they remained very poor for a long time and the public was sarcastic about their work, and even violently hostile. Auguste Renoir once said to his dealer, Ambroise Vollard, that, without Monet, they would all have given up.

Monet also seemed an extremist in the group. He went further than any other Impressionist in capturing the fleeting nature of time, and he explored the sensation of a moment to the point where the image became almost blurred and the subject matter barely recognizable.

Of the greatest Impressionists, Monet lived longest. Berthe Morisot died in 1895, Alfred Sisley in 1899, Camille Pissarro in 1903. Auguste Renoir, who, among the first dissidents, remained closest to the Impressionists, died in 1919. The two other dissidents were Paul Cézanne and Edgar Degas, who died in 1906 and 1917 respectively. Renoir and Monet were still alive when the twentieth century went through the upheavals

Portrait of Camille Monet, 1866-1867.   Charcoal
Private collection

of Fauvism in 1905, Cubism in 1908, and Dada in 1915.   Monet was still alive when André Breton published the "Surrealist Manifesto" in 1924.   When he died in 1926, Monet was the last of the great Impressionist painters: The Impressionist School, which had begun with Monet, Renoir, and Pissarro in particular, came to a close with Monet.

The first real Impressionist paintings date back to 1869, when Pissarro was working around Pontoise, and Renoir and Monet at La Grenouillère in Bougival.   Their canvases bear witness to the main technical characteristics of Impressionism: They painted in separate brushstrokes and pure tones, using black sparsely, without chiaroscuro, and they showed a preference for reflected light, especially light reflected off water.   For

years, Monet and his friends had held discussions on their ideas regarding art, and they may all be said to have played a part in the invention of Impressionism. Many elements of what became Impressionism already existed in the history of art.   The separate brushstrokes recall the multicolored fragments of stone in ancient mosaics.   More recently, John Constable and Eugène Delacroix, himself influenced by Constable, used separate brushstrokes juxtaposing different colors.   Among the precursors of Impressionism, Delacroix explored the problem of reflected light, observing that the color of an object can alter that of an object nearby, just as the color of an image is changed when reflected in a mirror.   The Impressionists were remarkable for their realism, but many other painters strove to paint only what they saw, such as Caravaggio, José Ribera, and the Le Nain brothers, or Gustave Courbet, whom the Impressionists knew personally and even admired.   The first critics to defend the Impressionists defined their art as "painting in light tints," believing that the Impressionists were the first to reject the use of chiaroscuro.   In point of fact,

Monsieur Orchard, 1856
Pencil, 12¾" × 9½" (32.5 × 24.2 cm)
The Art Institute, Chicago
Carter H. Harrison Collection

Studies, 1864
Black crayon, 7⅞″ × 8⅝″ (20 × 22 cm)
Private collection

▷

THE CRADLE - CAMILLE MONET
WITH THE ARTIST'S SON JEAN, 1867
Oil on canvas, 46″ × 35″ (116.8 × 88.9 cm)
National Gallery of Art, Washington, D.C.
Collection of Mr. and Mrs. Paul Mellon

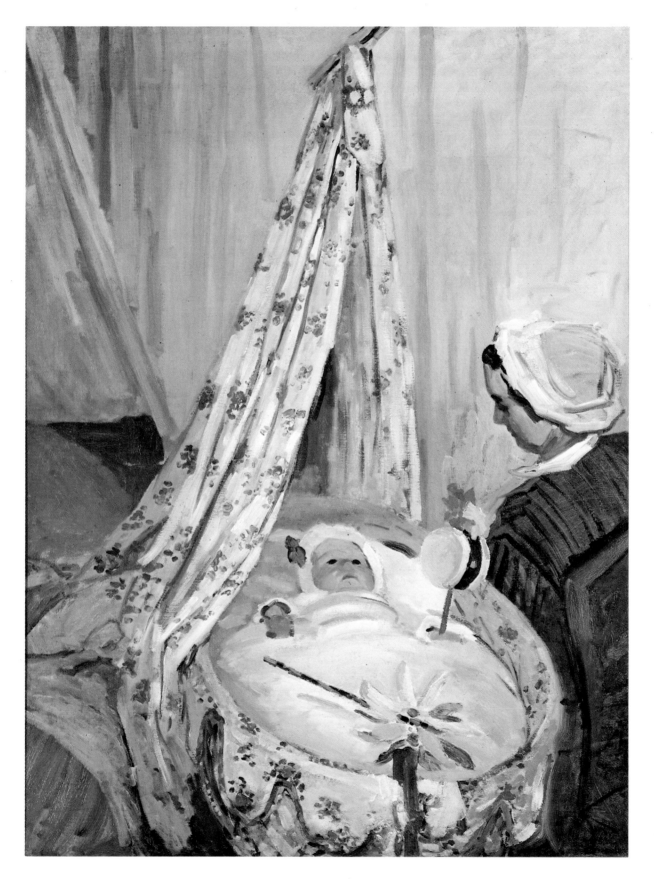

PORTRAIT OF BLANCHE HOSCHEDÉ-MONET, ca 1880.   Oil on canvas, 18⅛″ × 15″ (46 × 38 cm)
Musée des Beaux-Arts, Rouen

PORTRAIT OF MADAME GAUDIBERT, 1868. Oil on canvas, 85″ × 54⅜″ (216 × 138 cm)
Musée d'Orsay, Paris

The Luncheon, 1868.   Oil on canvas, 90⅜″ × 59⅛″ (230 × 150 cm)
Städelsches Kunstinstitut, Frankfurt

however, before them Courbet, Camille Corot, Johan Barthold Jongkind, and Eugène Boudin had already produced paintings bathed in light. There had even been light paintings in the sixteenth and seventeenth century. Paintings before the Renaissance feature very little shadow or none at all. Impressionism can hence be said to be less the invention of a new technique than the re-examination of approaches and techniques explored by many other artists throughout history. This re-examination was the work of a group of painters, and it would be impossible to single out one of them as responsible for the Impressionist style. Nevertheless, Monet played a major role in the development of such a style and he also took a decisive part in the creation of the movement. It was he who decided to organize the Impressionists' first exhibition, thus appearing to be the head of the group.

Léon Machon (the Notary), 1856
Charcoal, 23⅝" × 17¾" (60 × 45 cm)
The Art Institute, Chicago
Carter H. Harrison Collection

Already in 1863, as a young man, Monet felt dissatisfied with the conventional teaching he received at Gleyre's studio. He rounded up three like-minded fellow students, Auguste Renoir, Frédéric Bazille, and Alfred Sisley, proposing that they escape elsewhere on the grounds that honesty was impossible at Gleyre's school, where the atmosphere was unhealthy. Instead of taking them to another studio, he suggested they set out for the forest of Fontainebleau, where they began to paint in the open air. This in itself was not entirely new. There had been painters who had worked out of doors before. But it was a daring decision on the part of young painters, showing their unwillingness to conform. This was also the first step toward Impressionism. They sensed that a landscape painted outdoors — trees, rocks, ponds, mossy patches, an expanse of grass — is more likely to be realistic than when it is composed from sketches in a studio or at school. In the plein air, the stirring wind and shimmering light serve as models. They produce an impression — and Monet was to set great store upon this word — which may be lost if it is not captured on the spot. Even when the painter believes that he has not forgotten, his memory can be

SAINT-GERMAIN L'AUXERROIS, 1866
Oil on canvas, 31⅞″ × 39⅜″ (81 × 100 cm)
Staatliche Museen, Berlin
Federal Republic of Germany

THE GARDEN OF THE PRINCESS, 1867
Oil on canvas, 36⅛″ × 24⅜″ (91 × 62 cm)
Allen Memorial Art Museum, Oberlin, Ohio
R. T. Miller, Jr. Fund

▷

deceptive. Reality changes as it is remembered, certain aspects are rubbed out while others are emphasized. The painter fails to realize how much he has forgotten. Errors and inaccuracies grow in the memory, and they are embellished by subsequent events and conversations. Paintings by artists who see reality differently can persuade the viewer that he has seen a landscape as they have; if they saw shadows in the forest, the young painter begins to think that he, too, has seen them. Thus he betrays both the forest and himself. Monet led the group to the forest of Fontainebleau to make sure that they would avoid this double betrayal.

On another occasion, Monet and Renoir were working together in the studio that Bazille had lent them in his absence. The studio was on the Place Furstenberg, in Paris, opposite the one owned by Delacroix. Renoir and Monet greatly admired Delacroix and were always on the lookout for news about the aging master, whom Charles Baudelaire had called the leader of the Romantic School of painting. One day they saw a model enter his studio, to leave only a few minutes later. They were very puzzled by this, and after some discussion, they reached two possible conclusions — either Delacroix had studied the model and was to paint her at leisure from memory, or he had painted her very rapidly during the short time she had been at his studio. Delacroix died a few weeks later, before they were able to establish what, in fact, had happened in the studio. It was up to them to decide which of the alternatives was the more worthy of Delacroix. When, in 1874, we see Monet in his boat near Argenteuil, we know which alternative he chose.

THE RAPHAEL OF WATER

The man out for a walk along the Seine is still shading his eyes from the sun. He is watching as Monet draws his oars into the boat and reaches for a kind of stool on which he places a white rectangle 23¾" wide and 19¾" high. Monet then opens a box of paints, takes up a brush in his right hand, and places the thumb of his left hand in the hole inside his palette. In 1874, such tubes of oil paints were still a novelty, having appeared on the market for the first time in 1861. They greatly simplified a painter's work; they were much easier to carry than the powders of days gone by, which were difficult to work with outside the studio. It was now possible to start and complete a painting outdoors, even in a wind such as that blowing across the Seine that day.

Monet extends the legs of his portable easel and sets it up firmly. His white canvas shines in the sun. He was not the first artist to install an easel in a small boat. Nine years earlier, in 1865, his friends Renoir and Sisley had sailed down the Seine to watch

Hôtel des Roches Noires, Trouville, 1870.   Oil on canvas, 31½″ × 21⅝″ (80 × 55 cm)
Musée d'Orsay, Paris

Algerian Landscape, 1860-1862.   Black crayon, 5⅛″ × 8⅝″ (13 × 22 cm)
Formerly in the Michel Monet Collection, Giverny

a regatta at Le Havre.   On the way down, they had stopped to paint at all the places they had liked.   Even before them, François Daubigné had painted from his boat called "Botin."   He was a well-known landscape artist, whom the Impressionists had met while painting in the forest of Fontainebleau.   He was very helpful to them, especially on one occasion, when he persuaded the jury of the Salon to exhibit their works.

However, Monet's boat — which the stroller on the bank called "Monet's studio" [1] — suits his character more than it ever did that of other painters.   As a child at Le Havre, Monet had so often watched the ocean and admired the magic of water.   Although he was born in Paris, he spent his childhood and early manhood close to the sea.   Later he was to say that he wanted to spend his whole life by the sea or at sea, and be buried in a buoy after his death.   It was Eugène Boudin, himself a painter of "the wondrous magic of air and water," [2] who guessed that the young caricaturist whose satirical portraits were exhibited in the window of a paintshop had the makings of a great artist.

(1) *Monet's Floating Studio*, 1874, Bayerische Staatsgalerie, Munich.
(2) This is how Baudelaire described Boudin's paintings at the Salon of 1859 ("Art in Paris 1845-1862." Ed. and tr. by J. Mayne, Aberdeen, 1965).

26

At the time Monet was quite successful as a caricaturist, but he let himself be persuaded by Boudin to take up painting. Boudin and Jongkind, who was also a friend of Monet, were both among the most significant forerunners of the Impressionist School and they certainly encouraged Monet to try and depict water on canvas. It was this deep fascination which must have inspired Monet to paint his first Impressionist works at La Grenouillère. It must have been Monet who took Renoir along to paint the evermoving play of sunshine upon the surface of the water.

Monet was forever on the lookout for water. When he was away from the sea, he went in search of a river, a stream, or even canals. He loved Amsterdam, where he went in the early 1870s, and Venice, which he visited in 1908. At the end of his life, he happily painted the pond in his garden. He loved water in every form or shape, even when it turns into mist or smoke. The painting *Impression: Sunrise*, from which the word Impressionist was coined, is not only a seascape but also a study of morning mist. Between 1876 and 1878, he painted a series of works entitled *Gare Saint-Lazare* (see page 51), which are a study of smoke. In 1880, when he painted the thaw and

The Harbor at Touques, 1865. Charcoal. Private collection

BOATS IN LONDON HARBOR, 1871
Oil on canvas, 18½″ × 28¾″ (47 × 73 cm)
Galerie Schmit, Paris

THE REGATTA AT ARGENTEUIL, 1872
Oil on canvas, 18⅞″ × 29½″ (48 × 75 cm)
Musée d'Orsay, Paris

On the Seine at Bennecourt, 1868
Oil on canvas, 31⅞″ × 39½″ (81 × 100.3 cm)
The Art Institute, Chicago
Potter Palmer Collection

30

31

IMPRESSION: SUNRISE, 1872.   Oil on canvas, 18⅞″ × 24¹³⁄₁₆″ (48 × 63 cm)
Musée Marmottan, Paris

floating ice on the Seine (see page 62), he was again depicting water in one of its many aspects. His fascination with water was such that he painted leaves, grass, and meadows as he painted water, the brushstrokes like so many quivering waves in the air. Even the crowds on the *Boulevard des Capucines*, dated 1873,[3] resemble an ocean. Sometimes the trunks and branches of his trees are painted like rivers and streams flowing on a transparent surface. Monet did not limit himself to painting water. He also adopted a technique whereby he depicted everything with the same brushstroke he had used at the beginning of his Impressionist period to depict the shimmering movement of waves. For instance, the sky in Amsterdam seems to ripple (see page 50); the separate brushstrokes turn the houses into as many little waves. Trees spring forth like geysers. Even in portraits, the skin covering the most solid parts of a face is painted in small waves, such as the skin over the cheekbones in his 1917 *Self-Portrait*.[4] Auguste Rodin, who exhibited with Monet in 1889, used the same technique in sculpture, dividing up the surface into minute waves. This technique of separate brushstrokes helped Monet to achieve unique results, whereby he broke up the texture of matter, even dissolving stone. The most spectacular example is his series of paintings of *Rouen Cathedral* (see pages 70 and 71), in which the façade resembles water cascading from slits in the blue sky. A similar technique dissolves the stones of the *Houses of Parliament* in London (see page 72) and the *Palazzo da Mula* in Venice.[5]

Monet's treatment of the sky is even more significant. Here the process is reversed and instead of softening the texture of hard matter, he added texture to air and sky. The sky becomes a sort of ocean above the ocean. This is most evident in his Amsterdam landscapes and his *Houses of Parliament*. Monet's liquid sky was the intermediate stage between a more traditional rendering of sky and that hard, mineral sky characteristic of Cézanne's work. Like Cézanne, Monet rarely painted open space in a landscape. His distant views resemble liquid walls. In some cases he used a foreshortened downward perspective which cuts out the sky entirely from the painting. When, in the winter of 1885, he painted boats aground on the beach,[6] he set up his easel on a cliff and from this vantage point he could see, in addition to a few boats, a house on the beach and the sea spilling foam over the pebbles. He would have had to raise his head to see the sky, which does not appear in the painting. In *Palazzo da Mula*, dated 1908, only the canal and the lower part of the palace are featured; the sky is

(3) Atkins Museum, Kansas City.
(4) Musée d'Orsay. Paris.
(5) 1908, National Gallery of Art, Washington, D.C.
(6) *Boats in Winter Quarters, Etretat*, two paintings at the Art Institute, Chicago.

View of Rouen, 1872
Black crayon on white scratchboard
12⅞″ × 19¹³⁄₁₆″ (32.7 × 51.3 cm)
Sterling and Francine Clark Institute
Williamstown, Massachusetts

▷
Boats, n.d. Sketchbook No. 5128
Pencil
Musée Marmottan, Paris

34

hidden by walls. By 1921, Monet was able to dissolve all matter. Magically, his paintbrush could turn everything into water and by then he needed only to look at his garden. The sky appears in the *Water Lilies* (see pages 82-83), but as a reflection in the pond, and water seems to have taken over the whole canvas.

This fascination for water evokes some primeval myth in our culture as well as fundamental structures in our psyche. In this connection Monet's art belongs to a family of styles inspired by the world of plants and water — Gothic art and its cathedrals, which are forests of stone; Baroque art, with a leitmotiv of rising waves; finally, Art Nouveau, which drew both from the Gothic and the Baroque and developed between 1895 and 1910. Monet's art is utterly different from geometric, rational art, because its strength owes more to instinct than reason. He himself said that he painted as a bird sings, and this brought him close to the most instinctive among the Fauves, such as Maurice de Vlaminck. One day in 1901, a strapping young man — looking more like a prizefighter than an art connoisseur — walked into a gallery in Paris showing a

◁

Boats on a Beach, 1865
Pencil, 9″ × 12″ (23 × 30.5 cm)
Private collection

THE BEACH AT TROUVILLE, 1870
Oil on canvas, 14¹⁵⁄₁₆″ × 18⅛″ (38 × 46 cm)
The National Gallery, London

MADAME MONET IN THE GARDEN, ca 1872
Oil on canvas, 20¼" × 26" (51.5 × 66 cm)
Private collection
Courtesy of The Los Angeles County Museum of Art

THE LUNCHEON, ca 1873-1874
Oil on canvas, 63″ × 79⅛″ (160 × 201 cm)
Musée d'Orsay, Paris

THE RED CAPELINE - MADAME MONET, 1873.   Oil on canvas, 39⅜″ × 31½″ (100 × 80 cm)
The Cleveland Museum of Art. Bequest of Leonard C. Hanna, Jr.

retrospective of Vincent van Gogh. On leaving, he stated dramatically, "I love Van Gogh more than I love my own father." This was Vlaminck, and he could not have made so bombastic a statement if, earlier, he had not learned to love color from Monet's paintings. Vlaminck painted entirely from instinct, more so than Monet. But both were forerunners of Abstract Expressionism and, as such, their style was poles apart from geometric Abstractionism.

Monet's preoccupation with spontaneity stemmed from a leaning toward realism, which he had acquired from Courbet. However, the spontaneity which enables an artist "to paint as a bird sings" is difficult to achieve. Successive generations can contrive to improve upon it. Two years before Monet died, Surrealism appeared. However different Surrealism was from Impressionism in its goals and methods, the new movement upheld the idea of an artist painting as a bird sings, which developed into the technique of "automatic writing."

On that day at Argenteuil, a real bird began to sing above the man on the bank of the Seine, who raised his head and looked away from Monet's boat. When he looked back, he searched for a name to give the white-coated painter — it was to be "The Raphael of Water."

The symbolism of water in Monet's painting brings to mind the sea voyages of the second half of the nineteenth century, which were more easily undertaken and longer than hitherto. They changed man's preconceived ideas regarding the ocean and distant lands. Long sea voyages were no longer the prerequisite of specialists. The art critic Théodore Duret actually sailed around the world. Before him, Baudelaire had been to India. Pissarro came from the West Indies. Degas spent several months in New Orleans the year before the first Impressionist exhibition. Later Paul Gauguin sailed, as Cézanne put it, "over all the world's seas." Even the stroller watching Monet in his floating studio had, at the age of sixteen, sailed for Rio de Janeiro as an apprentice pilot on the vessel "Havre et Guadeloupe." Monet did not undertake such long voyages, but he crossed the Channel to London in 1870 and, a few months later, sailed across the North Sea to Holland. In 1883, he went with Renoir to visit Cézanne at Aix-en-Provence, and they traveled to the Mediterranean coast. The following year, he stayed at Bordighera on the Italian coast, where he painted studies of light and shade upon leaves and shimmering waves mirrored in the windows of houses on the shore. In 1886, he spent the fall and winter at Belle-Ile, off the coast of Brittany. In 1888 he painted at Antibes and Juan-les Pins, on the coast of Provence. In 1909, he discovered the Adriatic in Venice.

Windmills in Holland, n.d.
Sketchbook, p. 33. Pencil
Musée Marmottan, Paris

▷

Bridge in Holland, n.d.
Sketchbook, p. 32. Pencil
Musée Marmottan, Paris

In 1860, as a young soldier, Monet had crossed to Algeria on a cargo boat. He returned to France two years later. One cannot help but wonder whether these two crossings of the Mediterranean had as much influence on Monet as they had on Delacroix, whose voyage to Morocco and Algeria in 1832 had clearly been the most significant event in his life. Thirty years had elapsed since Delacroix's trip, and much had changed in the meantime. The very relationship to the sea had changed. Delacroix had already sensed this, but Monet recognized it more clearly. The sea itself seemed different — it was not so completely opposite to the land as it had been before. Blaise Pascal noted that rivers and streams connect people as much as roads; in a similar way, oceans and seas had become links between continents rather than obstacles separating them. The dissolved stones in Monet's work conveyed the idea that the polarity between stone and water could be abolished, just as the polarity between seas and continents had been abolished. Cézanne conveyed the same idea; the sea seems petrified in his pictures, and the Mediterranean takes on the aspect of an expanse of tar.

32

Harbor in Holland, n.d.   Sketchbook, p. 29.   Drawing.   Musée Marmottan, Paris

In the same manner, differences between people and distances separating civilizations seemed less great than they had been before.   Delacroix realized this when he traveled to North Africa in 1832, when North Africa was an area where Europeans had rarely set foot except as prisoners of the Moors.   It was then said that Europeans could only survive there as prisoners or as converts to Islam.   However, Delacroix was not forced to renounce his faith in order to travel freely through Morocco and Tunisia.   It was as if the two civilizations had ceased to be mutually incompatible.   Delacroix was not fully aware that antagonisms between people had been broken down, but, in another realm of thought, he noted in his diary his ideas on the optical relationship between visible objects.   In 1857 he wrote, "When we look at ordinary, everyday objects which we see around us in a landscape or a house, we notice that they are connected to each other by the atmosphere around them and that reflected light is the agent binding all things harmoniously together."   It was also Monet's ambition to bring out this

HOUSES ON THE ZAAN, ZAANDAM, 1871
Oil on canvas, 18¹¹⁄₁₆″ × 28¹⁵⁄₁₆″ (47.5 × 73.5 cm)
Städelsches Kunstinstitut, Frankfurt

connection between everything, a connection which stood as a symbol of the link between different civilizations and the gradual reduction of natural boundaries such as seas and oceans.

In 1860, Monet set out for North Africa. Fifteen years later, in 1872, he is back at Le Havre, in his room, where the window looks out on to the harbor. Dawn is breaking.

SUNRISE

The sun rises slowly in the mist enveloping Le Havre. Monet is watching the enchanting scene from behind his window. Water and fog create this unity out of diversity, which had meant so much to Delacroix, and the sun floats in the mist, as a symbol of the future yet unborn. This vision of a ball of light held captive within a misty, watery world was to haunt Monet until the end of his life, when, as an old man at Giverny, he would paint the reflection of clear sky in the yellowish green water of a pond in his garden.

But today Monet is still a young man of thirty-two, just starting out on his career as an Impressionist painter. The slowly rising sun becomes a symbol of his gradual mastery of clarity in art. No wonder that *Impression: Sunrise* should have caused a scandal at the time: It appeals to an aesthetic sensitivity which was less common in 1874, when the painting was exhibited, than it is nowadays. The incessant turmoils of modern life are such that we are swamped with pictures, colors, and sounds. We crave for peace and simplicity, and this painting epitomizes our needs. We see an orange-colored disk, three minute barges — one of which is barely visible — a few lines indicating waves, and a limited range of tints. This simplicity challenges our imagination. We feel it stir at the sight of the sun struggling to break through the mist, as Monet was stirred, and we gradually discover the richness of a seascape which had seemed so flat at first sight. Even the location of the warm-colored disk on the canvas is challenging. Monet painted the sun on the right hand-side of the picture, rather than in the center. It is just a tiny spot of color. It evokes the Japanese master engraver Hokusai, whose unfulfilled ambition was to produce a single dot so perfectly executed and situated on the page that it appeared to be alive. Monet knew the work of the Japanese engravers, since Mrs. de Soye had opened a shop called "La Jonque d'Or," in the Rue de Rivoli, in Paris, where, from 1862 on, she sold Chinese and Japanese art works to a growing number of collectors. In 1876 Monet painted a picture entitled *La Japonaise* (see page 57). The model in Japanese dress poses against a blue background decorated with fans.

Her attitude is similar to that of figures found in Japanese prints of the period.   By a curious coincidence, the painting by Monet which was to be instrumental in the coining of the word "Impressionism," was *Impression: Sunrise*, almost as an allusion to the word "engraving" and the "Empire of the Rising Sun."

Monet's prodigious ability to discover the infinite in the world around him also evokes Zen mysticism.   The art historian Elie Faure wrote aptly that, for Claude Monet, there are one hundred thousand possible images in the space of one second.   *Impression: Sunrise* is indeed a seascape at Le Havre composed of an infinite variety of elements.   At first, one can only see mist surrounding a spot of orange light.   On further observation the barges become noticeable, but at first only the largest of them.   There are two figures on board, one very carefully outlined.   This figure is rowing with a stern oar, leaving no doubt about the direction taken by the barge.   The second figure . . .   But is it really a figure, or a sack?   The second barge then captures one's attention; it carries three figures — or is it one oarsman and two sacks?   Or two oarsmen and one sack?   Or even three passengers and a small sail?   The third barge comes then to the fore.   It seems impossible to tell whether it is full or empty, still or moving, large or small.   While pondering, one may notice also that the three barges form a straight line, which

Cliff at Etretat, ca 1885.   Pastel, 8¼″ × 14½″ (21 × 37 cm)
Musée Marmottan, Paris.   Bequest of Michel Monet

CLIFF AT ETRETAT, 1868-1869
Oil on cavas, 31⅞″ × 38⅜″ (81 × 100 cm)
The Fogg Art Museum, Cambridge, Massachusetts
Gift of Mr. and Mrs. Joseph Pulitzer, Jr.

THE MANNEPORTE, HIGH SEAS, 1885
Oil on canvas, 24⅝″ × 32⅜″ (65 × 81.3 cm)
Mr. and Mrs. A. N. Pritzker
Courtesy of The Los Angeles County Museum of Art

THE DRAWBRIDGE, AMSTERDAM, 1874
Oil on cavas, 21⅛″ × 25″ (53 × 63.5 cm)
The Shelburne Museum, Shelburne, Vermont

50

THE EUROPE BRIDGE AT SAINT-LAZARE TRAIN STATION, 1877
Oil on canvas, 25⅜" × 31⅞" (64 × 81 cm)
Musée Marmottan, Paris
Bequest of Mrs. Donop de Monchy

PARISIANS ENJOYING THE PARC MONCEAU, 1878.   Oil on canvas, 28⅝″ × 21⅜″ (72.7 × 54.3 cm)
The Metropolitan Museum of Art, New York. Mr. and Mrs. Henry Ittleson Fund

would cross at an angle the line drawn by the reflection of the sun in the water. The careful arrangement of these lines with the orange spot and various other points on the canvas create several triangles. And a host of geometric shapes are outlined by the many lines drawn from shapes which become gradually more visible in the mist — reflections, sails, masts, and cranes. This is quite surprising in so hazy a scene. Then one's attention turns to the colors. The sea is not the same bluish gray shade all over: It is green in certain parts of the picture, yellowish or purple elsewhere. The sky is painted in different reddish hues. Finally, the waves are not uniform horizontal lines; some lines are thick, others thin, some short, some long, some seem still, others seem as quick as a shoal of fish. What had appeared to be a very simple painting reveals a composition made of elements too numerous to be counted, thus proving Elie Faure's observation to be correct. There is infinity in Monet's paintings, but they are so deceptively simple that the viewer needs the greatest care to see it, and his attentive observation must match Monet's own.

Many different thoughts may have come to Monet's mind while he was sitting by his easel near the window of his room in Le Havre, watching the misty sunrise over the harbor. When his thoughts recede and his mind quiets within him, he takes up his brush and palette. Before he starts working, he must ensure that he will be able to detect everything — not only the slightest movement in the morning haze, but also these tiny reflections on his window panes, which change his view of the harbor and are painted on the canvas. He is watching everything with the greatest care.

While the man by the Seine near Argenteuil is observing him, as he is squatting down on the deck of his floating studio — like the tiny sage in a skiff featured at the bottom of a tall Chinese or Japanese wash drawing — Monet holds his brushes in his right hand and his palette in his left. The canvas shines white before him. He is not painting; here again, he is watching with the greatest care. He may be thinking of a visit he paid to Paris two years previously with his friend Boudin. He was little more than a child when he first met Boudin. He was drawing caricatures at the time, but even then his power of observation was well developed. Nothing escaped him: the slightest defect in a face, the trace of a grin, a drooping eyelid, a bump on the nose, the pursing of the lips, the curve of eyelashes, and the curls in a beard or a mustache (see pages 15 and 21). Boudin persuaded him to take up painting, and Monet became a landscape artist. Since Boudin kept painting the sky, the sea, and beaches — water and light — Monet came to the realization that outdoor light is essentially different from indoor light because of its intensity, diffusion, and mobility. But how can one paint moving light?

Two Men Fishing, ca 1882
Black crayon on scratchboard
10" × 13½" (25.5 × 34.4 cm)
The Fogg Art Museum, Cambridge, Massachussets
Bequest of Meta and Paul J. Sachs

▷

Meadow Edged with Trees, n.d.
Pastel with gouache highlights
8⅝" × 14⁹⁄₁₆" (22 × 37 cm)
Musée Marmottan, Paris
Bequest of Michel Monet

He found the answer in 1860, when for the first time he met the man whom he and Boudin had just visited in Paris. Courbet was then the leader of the Realist School. In 1871 he was imprisoned for his alleged participation in the demolition of the Colonne Vendôme during the Commune, the 1870-1871 revolution in Paris. Monet felt sympathy, friendly admiration, even gratitude toward Courbet. It was Courbet who had taught him something which set him apart from the other Impressionists. Like Courbet, he painted mostly with vigorous brushstrokes, as can be seen in *Side of Beef*, dated 1864,[7] in the pelt of the dog held by Camille in a portrait dated 1866,[8] in the headdress of the woman looking at Jean Monet in his cradle (see page 17), the grass on which the woman is sitting, by the Seine at Bennecourt (see page 30). In 1869, Renoir and Monet painted the same boats moored by a bathing establishment on the Seine, the same shimmering water. Renoir's brushstroke is round and soft,[9] Monet's is straight and energetic, closer to Courbet's manner (see page 31).[10] The same

(7) Musée d'Orsay, Paris.
(8) Private collection.
(9) Renoir painted three views of *La Grenouillère*. They are at the Nationalmuseum, Stockholm; the Pushkin Museum of Fine Arts in Moscow; and the Reinhart Collection in Winterthur, Switzerland.
(10) There are two other versions of *Bathing at La Grenouillère* by Monet. One was in the collection of Manet and is now at the Metropolitan Museum of Art, New York. The other one was formerly in a private collection in Berlin.

Woman with a Parasol, 1866
Pencil, 20⅞″ × 16⅛″ (53 × 41 cm)
Private collection

energetic brushstroke is apparent in *The Beach at Trouville* (see page 37), *The Regatta at Argenteuil* (see page 29), and *Boats in Winter Quarters: Etretat* (1885). Toward the end of his life, Monet still used wide brushstrokes to paint the breathtaking colors and curving lines of weeping willows (see page 80).

These wide brushstrokes seem to impart a changing quality to the picture, whereby it looks different according to distance. When it is viewed from close by, the picture is made of a mysterious texture streaked with hair from the brush. When it is seen from a distance, the same matter becomes fat in a side of beef, grass on the banks of the river, or folds in a headdress. It creates an element of surprise, which is so important for any aesthetic appreciation. Toward the end of Monet's life, this wide brushstroke did not change even when seen from a distance—it did not change into grass, fabric, or reflecte light. Color simply remained color, as if Monet pointed to the fact that we cannot expect to recognize everything in the world around us. Familiar objects may seem hardly recognizable, such as the *Weeping Willows* painted around 1918, which seem more like geysers, green flames, or waterfalls than trees. Unlike modern contemporary artists, who produce abstract paintings while drawing their inspiration from nature, Monet was not purposefully searching for that which is ambiguous. He also did not avoid it, but saw it as worth painting. Using Courbet's wide brushstroke, he honed a technique which enabled him better to capture the fleeting aspect of reality. The quick, wide brushwork was perfectly adapted for this brief moment when the eye does not yet recognize that which it can register. This was Monet's own solution to the problem of depicting movement.

La Japonaise (Camille Monet in Japanese Costume), 1875
Oil on canvas, 91¼″ × 56″ (231 × 142.3 cm).   Museum of Fine Arts, Boston

WOMAN WITH A PARASOL (PLEIN-AIR STUDY OF A FIGURE TURNED TO THE RIGHT), 1886
Oil on canvas, 51⅝″ × 34⅝″ (131 × 88 cm)
Musée d'Orsay, Paris

WOMAN WITH A PARSOL. MADAME MONET AND HER SON, 1875
Oil on canvas, 39⅜″ × 31⅞″ (100 × 81 cm)
National Gallery of Art, Washington, D.C. Collection of Mr. and Mrs. Paul Mellon

Poppy Field at Argenteuil, 1873
Oil on canvas, 19⅝″ × 25⁹⁄₁₆″ (50 × 65 cm)
Musée d'Orsay, Paris

THE ARTIST'S FLOATING STUDIO, 1876
Oil on canvas, 21¼″ × 25⅝″ (54 × 65 cm)
Musée d'Art et d'Histoire, Neuchâtel, Switzerland
Bequest of Yvan and Hélène Amez-Droz

FLOATING ICE, 1880
Oil on canvas, 38³⁄₁₆″ × 59¼″ (97 × 150.5 cm)
The Shelburne Museum, Shelburne, Vermont

VAL DE LA FALAISE, 1885
Oil on canvas, 28¾″ × 36¼″ (73 × 92 cm)
Galerie Schmit, Paris

POPPY FIELD IN A HOLLOW NEAR GIVERNY, 1885
Oil on canvas, 25⅝″ × 32″ (65.2 × 81.2 cm)
Museum of Fine Arts, Boston. Juliana Cheney Edwards Collection
Bequest of Robert J. Edwards in memory of his mother

THE INVENTION OF COLOR

The wind has dropped. The little boats cruising near Monet's floating studio come to a stop and the reflection of their sails is just perceptible in the rise and fall of the water. The man on the bank of the Seine erects the wooden contraption that he has just laid in the grass. There is movement in the boat; Monet raises his right arm, and there follow in quick succession one — two — three — four — forty — one hundred strokes of the brush. Very quickly, his white canvas is covered with light shades of color. Monet accomplishes in a few minutes what others would have done in several days or even weeks.

According to Baudelaire, Delacroix replied one day to a young man seeking his advice, "Sir, if you are unable to paint a workman as he is falling off a roof, you are not capable of much." Monet did not paint workmen falling off a roof but the reflection of shimmering sails in the water, which can be destroyed by a mere breath of wind. He could rely on his memory and imagination to capture this fleeting moment, but he refused to paint from memory. Courbet had said emphatically, "I paint only what I can see. I have never seen an angel so I shall never paint one," and for twenty years he had shocked everybody with his realism. The aging Jean-Dominique Ingres once said bitterly of Courbet, "He is nothing more than one big eye." Years went by, and Cézanne said of Monet, "He is nothing more than an eye — but what an eye!" A glance at *The Regatta at Argenteuil* (see page 29) reveals at once Courbet's influence on Monet. Even the energetic movement of the hand evokes Courbet's manner; each brushstroke is squarely applied to the canvas, a solid and dense touch of color. Like Courbet, Monet was self-assured, clearly aware of his gift and purpose. Both were deeply convinced of the need for realism. Whenever the need for an ideal was mentioned to him, Courbet thought of something shockingly repulsive to paint. One might wonder at such a rage. It was because Courbet regarded an idea as being far poorer than reality, the latter holding more significance and mystery. He followed the development of Monet's technique with impassioned interest. When, in 1865, Monet painted the portrait of his friend Bazille, Courbet was there to watch his disciple at work. Monet painted his *Picnic Lunch* in the forest of Fontainebleau (see pages 10 and 11), and Courbet again was there to discuss techniques. On another occasion, in 1867, Monet was sitting on the edge of a trench he had dug in his garden in order to paint the upper part of a large canvas more easily. Courbet arrived on the scene, apparently unimpressed by the trench, but very surprised to see Monet doing nothing in front of a painting of four women in light dress among the leaves. He asked in a scolding tone, "What are you doing sitting there — why not work rather than twiddle your thumbs? There is

HAYSTACKS, END OF SUMMER, MORNING, 1891
Oil on canvas, 23¹³⁄₁₆″ × 39⅜″ (60.5 × 100 cm)
Musée d'Orsay, Paris

HAYSTACKS, END OF SUMMER, EVENING, 1891
Oil on canvas, 23⅝″ × 39⅜″ (60 × 100 cm)
The Art Institute, Chicago
Collection Arthur M. Wood
In memory of Pauline Palmer Wood

a lot to do to the picture yet." But Monet shook his head, "No, I am waiting for the sun." A cloud had temporarily veiled the sun and altered the intensity of light and shadow. Suddenly the whole scene seemed flat in a dimmed light. The shadow had vanished on the skirt of the woman sitting holding a parasol. Monet needed the full sunshine to see clearly the outline of shadows (see page 12). Later Berthe Morisot was to say of Monet's work, "Whenever I look at one of his paintings, I know instinctively which way to point my sunshade." His paintings are full of details showing the orientation of light and shadows, thus indicating the position of the sun in the sky and the time of day. And Courbet could only feel sympathy for Monet's preoccupation with the exact reproduction of light. Recently, as a visitor congratulated him on a beautiful seascape he had painted he had frowned. "The sea — the sea?" he asked, "I did not paint the sea — it was one o'clock do you understand? One o'clock!"

Although he was in favor of painting landscapes out of doors, Courbet disapproved of doing portraits outside the studio. He felt that features need to be painted with

Haystacks. Pencil, 5⅞" × 9⁷⁄₁₆" (15 × 24 cm). Private collection

THE VALLEY OF THE CREUSE, SUNSET, 1889.   Oil on canvas, 28¾″ × 27⁹⁄₁₆″ (73 × 70 cm)
Musée d'Unterlinden, Colmar, France

ROUEN CATHEDRAL: MAIN ENTRANCE, FULL SUNLIGHT, 1894
Oil on canvas, 42⅛″ × 28¾″ (107 × 73 cm)
Musée d'Orsay, Paris

ROUEN CATHEDRAL: SUNSET, 1894.   Oil on canvas, 39⅝″ × 26″ (100.5 × 66.2 cm)
Museum of Fine Arts, Boston. Juliana Cheney Edwards Collection
Bequest of Hannah Marcy Edwards in memory of her mother

HOUSES OF PARLIAMENT, SUNSET, 1903
Oil on canvas, 30″ × 36″ (76.2 × 91.5 cm)
Private collection
Courtesy Acquavella Galleries, New York

TWILIGHT, S. GIORGIO MAGGIORE, 1908
Oil on canvas, 25″ × 31⅞″ (63.5 × 81 cm)
National Museum of Wales, Cardiff

73

Boats on the Thames, 1902
Black crayon
Private collection

▷

Waterloo Bridge, ca 1900
Pastel, 11¾" × 18½" (30 × 47 cm)
Musée Marmottan, Paris
Bequest of Michel Monet

74

great care and that the steady light of the studio is essential. Unlike Courbet, who saw them as separate, Monet wanted to unite nature and man. For Monet, it is the same light that shines on women in a garden, on their footprints in the sand, on the grass, and the branches. For Courbet, as for the primitive and classical painters, a certain hierarchy must rule the different themes chosen by the artist. In Byzantine and Romanesque art, pride of place was given to the depiction of man — or God as a human figure. Landscapes were of little significance until the period before and during the Renaissance. The human figure, however, remained the most important theme throughout Western art, until the Impressionists abolished its preeminence over landscape. This different relationship between man and nature was explored further by Cézanne and the Cubists. Later the Abstractionists eliminated the representation of the human figure itself, painting enigmatic landscapes without horizon or depth of perspective. Chinese and Japanese artists seem to have been more preoccupied than Western artists had been until the Impressionists with this problem of the relationship between man and nature, and they came upon a solution close to that of the Impressionists, by which man became part of the landscape.

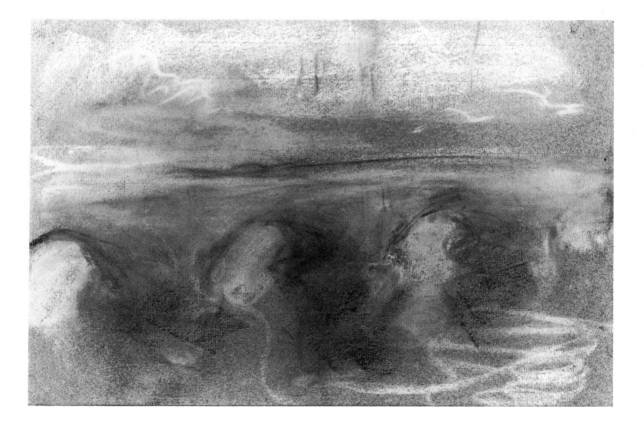

THE WATER LILY POND, 1904
Oil on canvas, 34½″ × 35¾″ (89.2 × 92.3 cm)
Denver Art Museum, Colorado
The Helen Dill Collection

▷

WATER LILIES, EVENING, 1907
Oil on canvas, 39⅜″ × 28¾″ (100 × 73 cm)
Musée Marmottan, Paris
Bequest of Michel Monet

*Monet Before the Small Bridge in Autumn, ca 1922. Photograph
Courtesy of Service Photographique de la Réunion des Musées Nationaux, Paris*

Soon after my arrival in Japan, I heard Japanese intellectuals mention a fundamental idea which can be expressed in two words — *sabi* and *wabi*. The nearest approximation in English of these two words is — rust and the hermit's solitude. The deep meaning of these two words also evokes Monet's work and personality. He was taciturn by nature: an all-seeing eye and a man of few words. It does not come as a surprise that he first worked as a caricaturist, revealing a streak of cruelty stemming from a feeling that there was no common ground between the people from Le Havre, whom he ridiculed, and himself. What the Japanese called rust made Monet more humane later on. The light in his paintings acted as rust — it smoothed and rounded the edges, it grounded matter into a dust of colored flecks, or dissolved an outline into tiny waves. In this process the boundaries between man and its surroundings disappeared. The figures were no longer men or women; they became part of the atmosphere surrounding them, the ground on which they stood. This made for another major difference between Courbet and Monet. When I first saw Courbet's pictures, I was troubled by what I took to be an error of judgment. I could not identify it exactly, but gradually and by dint of careful examination I reached the conclusion that Courbet's figures are not really standing — or lying — on the ground. They may be as little as a hair above the ground, but as a result *The Young Women on the Banks of the Seine* [11] are not really lying on the grass, and Mr. Bruyas's shoes in *Good Day, Mr. Courbet* [12] are not really touching the sand. Monet's figures, however, are always firmly grounded, and there is a continuity between man and all the elements that surround him.

In order to reach man an artist must depict the universe, in which everything is clearly connected. In Courbet's paintings — as in most Western art before the Impressionists — accurate flesh tones and correct anatomy sufficed to create a feeling of recognition in the viewer. Human relations in the West are based on a sort of physical recognition, while in the East this concept is almost entirely unknown. It seems at times that, instead of being born in Paris and raised in Le Havre, Monet might have been brought up in China or Japan. He is working on his boat at Argenteuil as speedily as those Japanese artists who can cover vast surfaces of paper in less than fifteen seconds. Eastern artists strive to achieve lightning speed in order to capture a fleeting vital energy. While painting, they must avoid any intellectual process, which might interrupt a burst of inspiration or slacken their creative impulse. In the same manner, Monet did not want his vision to be altered by thoughts. This is the reason why he said that he painted like a bird sings.

(11) 1856, Musée du Petit-Palais, Paris.
(12) 1854, Musée de Montpellier, France.

WILLOWS AT GIVERNY, ca 1918. Oil on canvas, 51¼″ × 60″ (127.6 × 152.4 cm)
Private collection. Courtesy of Acquavella Galleries, New York

Monet and Gustave Geffroy.   Photograph taken by Sacha Guitry, ca 1920
Courtesy of Service Photographique de la Réunion des Musées Nationaux, Paris

WATER LILIES, 1920-1921
Oil on canvas, 77^{15}/$_{16}$″ × 234^{7}/$_{8}$″ (198 × 596.6 cm)
Museum of Art, Carnegie Institute, Pittsburgh, Pennsylvania
Acquired through the generosity of Mrs. Alan M. Scaife

Boudin Working in Le Havre
Early pencil drawing, 11¹³/₁₆" × 8⅝" (30 × 22 cm)
Musée Eugène Boudin, Honfleur

Monet's treatment of color is very different from that of Eastern artists — particularly Japanese artists — for Japanese woodcuts in bright colors are an exception rather than the rule. The painter and art critic André Lhote called Monet "The Inventor of Color." One might wonder whether he was a painter of color or of light? It is true that the large series of *Water Lilies* on view in Paris create an impression of color more than light.[13] In the *Houses of Parliament* series, it is again a matter of colors: purples, oranges, and greens (see page 72). In *Twilight over Venice*, yellow breaks out in the midst of the blue and purple within the yellow.[14] Although Monet painted some extraordinary studies of light, such as *Woman with a Parasol* (see pages 58 and 59), these works are an exception. He did not approve of the Post-Impressionists Georges Seurat and Paul Signac, nor of the Pointillist efforts of Pissarro, who was haunted by light so bright that it outshone his colors. Monet could never accept that light should make one forget color.

Like the other Impressionists, Monet was motivated by a need for open-air light. At first, he depicted the intensity of light through the contrast between light and dark tints, as in the *Portrait of Camille Monet with a Dog* and *The Picnic Lunch* (see pages 10 and 11).[15] Such contrasts, however, presented one major drawback: Monet could not portray the diffuse, all-embracing quality of plein air light. And this is where he

(13) 1916-1923, Musée de l'Orangerie, Paris.
(14) 1908, Bridgestone Gallery, Tokyo.
(15) This painting was never completed. The left and central panels are now at the Musée d'Orsay in Paris, but the right-hand panel seems to be lost. The central panel held a prominent place in Monet's studio at Giverny. After Monet's death, it remained in a private collection, until it was recently bequeathed to the Musee d'Orsay. A very detailed study, dated 1866, is in the collection of the Pushkin Museum of Fine Arts in Moscow.

Monet Touching up a Painting in His Studio, 1920.   Photograph
Courtesy of Service Photographique de la Réunion des Musées Nationaux, Paris

WISTERIA, ca 1920
Oil on canvas, 39⅜″ × 118½″ (100 × 301 cm)
Musée Marmottan, Paris

was an innovator: Rather than drawing the intensity of light from contrasts, Monet created this intensity by juxtaposing areas of light. He looked everywhere for opportunities to paint light next to light, outdoors as well as indoors. That was the time when his son was born. Little Jean lay in his cradle, serious under the gaze of a woman with a white bonnet. Monet noticed the wealth of light colors in the cradle, the sheets, the woman's headdress, the baby's toys, and the nursery's walls. And he set to work (see page 17). *The Luncheon* shows the same pattern: Bright sun penetrates the thin curtains across the window; the white tablecloth, the child's napkin, his blond head, the straw on the chairs, the rug, and the maid's headdress make a symphony of light tints, although Monet has to leave some parts of the room dark (see page 20). *Madame Gaudibert* is painted in light tints against a light background (see page 19). Had he been a painter in chiaroscuro, Monet would have replaced the light blue curtain by a dark cloth, so as to bring out Madame Gaudibert's luminous silhouette. But Monet was of the opinion that greater intensity and truer light could be achieved by juxtaposing light tints rather than contrasting them with shadows. He went even further and attempted to do away with relief. Volumes were created by shafts of light balanced by shadows. These shadows, however, limit the space allotted to light on the canvas. He therefore tried to eliminate the shadows completely, as in the women's dresses in *Beach at Trouville* (see page 37), where there is almost no relief, and in *The Picnic Lunch*.

The Picnic Lunch is a title which is not really Monet's but had been used by another famous painter of the time. And while Monet was at work painting the Seine at Argenteuil, the man on the bank had put up his easel and was painting Monet's boat. When he finished, he signed the canvas "Manet."

Monet owed much to Manet. It was from Manet that Monet took his bold color planes. Manet had been the first artist in the West to have almost entirely ignored volumes, particularly in *The Picnic Lunch* and *Olympia*; [16] but he was still relying on contrasts between light and shadow, painting dark figures on a light background, or vice versa. When the pupil became a master, it was Monet who was to inspire Manet. On that day on the riverbank at Argenteuil Manet painted Monet and his boat in the Impressionist manner. The Impressionists substituted colors for shadows, and this was not entirely new, since Rubens and some mosaicists had also done so. The

(16) Musée d'Orsay, Paris.

THE PATH AT GIVERNY, 1922-1925
Oil on canvas, 28¾″ × 42″ (73 × 106.7 cm)
Private collection
Courtesy of Acquavella Galleries, New York

*Monet, Ker-Xavier Roussel, and Edouard Vuillard, 1920. Photograph
Courtesy of Service Photographique de la Réunion des Musées Nationaux, Paris*

Impressionists' major innovation was to paint light as it was reflected from one object to another and altered the colors of the objects themselves, challenging the notion one might have about the true color of things. Everything changed according to its surroundings. The Impressionists made a unique usage of reflections, linking shapes to one another as never before and putting less emphasis on composition. This is quite apparent from the comparison between the *Portrait of Madame Gaudibert*, dated 1868, and the one of *Madame Hoschedé-Monet*, dated 1880. There is practically no reflected light in the portrait of Madame Gaudibert (see page 19). Shapes are clearly outlined in a luminous atmosphere, and Monet puts together a beautiful arrangement with a table, a woman standing, her dress shaped as a cone, and the flat surface of a wall. He does this extremely well, but Madame Gaudibert needs to hold her right hand in such a way as to create a symmetry with her white collar. She stands in a three-quarter position so that the curve of her shoulder continues the line in the fold of the blue curtain. The portrait is staged, the result of a careful composition. Much later, when he painted the portrait of his daughter-in-law, Blanche Hoschedé-Monet, Monet did not need such an elaborate arrangement (see page 18). Reflected light holds the painting together. The light is still intense but forms and colors blend. Shadows do not create contrasts that must be measured carefully. Her nose projects a red shadow in a rose-colored face. Everything becomes beautiful, everything fits, everything becomes harmonious.

However, there could be an excess of harmony, as a result of which the viewer takes this harmony for granted or, worse, becomes unaware of it. And this is where Monet became a true innovator. The first great colorist of the nineteenth century had been Delacroix, whom Monet admired and of whom Baudelaire often remarked that he was a colorist *par excellence*. His colors, however, were still subdued by chiaroscuro. The Impressionists, and Monet among them, abolished the chiaroscuro. They discovered that colors are not only the components of light; they also have their own power and brilliance, different from that of simple light. Van Gogh understood this, when he noted that he wanted reds and greens to express passions. On closer examination, the *Portrait of Madame Hoschedé-Monet* reveals that Monet freed color from the chiaroscuro, but also from light itself, as if the colors needed to be freed from a misleading and shiny gangue. He created works which achieved an almost excessive harmony of colors, and this very excess imbues them with something vaguely disquieting. Through the magic of their colors, Monet's paintings are not simply an optimistic reflection of a world without shadows; they become a mysterious depiction of the power of life.

*Monet in His Studio with the Duke of Trévise Before the Central Panel
of "The Picnic Lunch," 1920. Photograph
Courtesy of Service Photographique de la Réunion des Musées Nationaux, Paris*

BIOGRAPHY

1840 Oscar Claude Monet was born in Paris on November 14. His father was a grocer.

1845 His family settled in Le Havre.

1856-58 Became a successful caricaturist. He met Eugène Boudin, whose work he did not like at first. However, Boudin convinced him to try painting landscapes.

1858 Took part for the first time in an art show.

1859 Failed to get a scholarship to study painting. With his family's help he settled in Paris, where he enrolled at the Académie Suisse. It was there, probably, that he met Camille Pissarro. His friend Armand Troyon introduced him into Realist circles.

1861-62 Military service in Algeria. He returned to Le Havre. Met Johan Berthold Jongkind, who had a great influence upon him.

1862-63 Return to Paris. He enrolled in Charles Gleyre's studio, where he met Frédéric Bazille, Auguste Renoir, and Alfred Sisley.

1864 Painted in the forest in Fontainebleau and at Barbizon. Stay at Honfleur with Bazille, Boudin, and Jongkind.

1865 Two landscapes at the Salon. He started working on the *Picnic Lunch*, which drew praise from Gustave Courbet. The painting was left unfinished.

1866 *Portrait of Camille (with a Green Dress)* was accepted at the Salon and praised by Emile Zola. Monet met Edouard Manet and started work on *Women in the Garden*.

1867 Rejected by the Salon. Camille Doncieux gave birth to his eldest son, Jean.

1868 One painting at the Salon. Stay at Etretat and Fécamp, where he attempted suicide. He was helped through his financial difficulties by his patrons in Le Havre, the Gaudiberts. Awarded a silver medal at the International Maritime Exhibition in Le Havre.

1869 Rejected by the Salon. He painted with Renoir near Bougival.

1870 Rejected by the Salon. He married Camille Doncieux. In the summer, after the Franco-Prussian war broke out, he and his family took refuge in England. There, he met up with Pissarro and was introduced to the dealer Paul Durand-Ruel.

1871 Trip to Holland with François Daubigny. At the end of the year, he returned to France and settled in Argenteuil.

1872 Stay in Rouen and Le Havre and second trip to Holland. He drew his inspiration mainly from the Seine and sailboats near Argenteuil.

1874 First Impressionist exhibition: Monet took part with twelve paintings, among which *Impression: Sunrise*.

1876 Second Impressionist Exhibition. Monet showed *La Japonaise* and several Argenteuil landscapes.

1877 Third Impressionist Exhibition. Monet showed views of *Saint-Lazare Train Station*.

1878 Moved to Paris then to Vétheuil. His son Michel was born.

1879 Fourth Impressionist Exhibition. Camille Monet died on September 5.

1880 *Lavacourt* was exhibited at the Salon. Monet did not show at the Fifth Impressionist Exhibition. Worked on the theme of the spring thaw. In June he had his first one-man show at the Galerie La Vie Moderne in Paris.

1881 Stay at Fécamp, Trouville, and Saint-Adresse. Durand-Ruel started to buy his paintings on a regular basis. In December he settled with Alice Hoschedé (the widow of one of his patrons), and their respective children at Poissy.

1882 Took part in the Seventh Impressionist Exhibition.

1883 Painted at Etretat. In March he had a one-man show at Durand-Ruel's gallery in Paris. He left Poissy for Giverny.

1884 Stay on the Mediterranean coast of Italy and France. He returned to Etretat in August.

1885 Took part in the Fourth International Exhibition at the Galerie Georges Petit in Paris. In the fall he moved to Etretat, where he remained until March 1886. In Etretat he often met up with Guy de Maupassant.

1886 Fifth International Exhibition. He sent ten paintings at the XX Exhibition in Brussels. Durand-Ruel showed forty of his paintings in New York. Short stay in Holland. Fall and winter at Belle-Ile, off the coast of Brittany.

1887 Sixth International Exhibition. Short stay in London in August. His first sale to Boussod & Valadon, through Théo van Gogh.

1888 Painted at Antibes and Juan-les-Pins. Ten of the Mediterranean paintings were exhibited at Boussod & Valadon's. Brief stay in London in July. He refused to be awarded the Legion of Honor.

1889 Stay at Fresselines, in the Creuse Valley. Successful retrospective at the Galerie Georges Petit. Monet showed three paintings at the Centennial Exhibition of French Art in Paris. He organized a subscription to buy Manet's *Olympia* for presentation to the French National Collection. Started work on the *Haystacks* series.

1890 He bought Giverny, where he built a new studio and started improvements on the garden.

1891 Exhibition at Durand-Ruel's, with fifteen *Haystacks*. Started his series on the *Poplars*. Trip to London in the autumn.

1892 Exhibition at Durand-Ruel's: *Poplars*. In the spring he started working on the *Rouen Cathedral* series. In July he married Alice Hoschedé.

1893 Started building the water lily pond at Giverny.

1894 Exhibition of his views of London. Paul Cézanne visited him at Giverny.

1895 Trip to Norway. Exhibition at Durand-Ruel's in May: twenty *Rouen Cathedrals*.

1896 Painted at Pourville and Varengeville. These works were exhibited in 1898 at Georges Petit's.

1899 First series on the garden at Giverny, the pond and

the Japanese bridge. Trip to London in the autumn.

1900 Trip to London in February. Durand-Ruel exhibited ten *Water Lilies* in Paris in the winter, then in New York the following year.

1901 Trip to London in the spring.

1902 Bought more land to further improve on the garden at Giverny. Bernheim-Jeune in Paris exhibited six landscapes of Vétheuil.

1903 Starded a second series on the water lily pond. Continued work on the Thames series.

1904 Exhibition at Durand-Ruel's: thirty-seven *Views of the Thames*. Trip to Spain in October to see paintings by Velásquez, followed by a stay in London.

1908 Fall and winter in Venice, where he studied effects of light and mist. His eyesight began failing.

1909 Exhibition at Durand-Ruel's: forty-eight *Water Lilies*.

1911 Alice Monet died in May.

1912 Exhibition at Bernheim-Jeune's: twenty-nine views of Venice. He was diagnosed as having cataracts.

1914 His son Jean (who had married Blanche Hoschedé in June 1897) died suddenly in February. Monet started building a new studio more suitable for very large canvases.

1922 Donated his largest *Water Lilies* to the French National Collection, thus keeping the promise he had made to Georges Clémenceau when the war ended in 1918.

1923 Underwent surgery for cataracts, which partially restored his eyesight.

1924 Exhibition at Durand-Ruel's in New York: *Water Lilies*. Large retrospective show at Georges Petit's in Paris.

1926 Edouard Vuillard and Ker-Xavier Roussel visited Monet at Giverny. He died at Giverny on December 5.

BIBLIOGRAPHY

ADHÉMAR, Hélène. *Claude Monet.* Paris: Chêne, 1950.

AITKEN, Geneviève. *La Collection d'estampes japonaises de Claude Monet à Giverny.* Paris: Bibliothèque des Arts, 1983.

ALEXANDRE, Arsène. *Claude Monet.* Paris: Bernheim-Jeune, 1921.

BESSON, Georges. *Monet.* Paris: Braun, 1951.

CETTO, A. M. *Claude Monet.* Basel, 1943, 1947.

CLÉMENCEAU, Georges. *Claude Monet: Les Nymphéas.* Paris: Plon, 1928. *Claude Monet: The Water Lilies.* Garden City, New York: Doubleday, 1930. Reissued as *Claude Monet: Cinquante ans d'amitié.* Paris, Geneva: Palatine, 1965.

DEGAND, L. and ROUART, D. *Claude Monet.* Geneva, 1958.

DUFWA, Jacques. *Winds from the East: A Study in the Art of Manet, Degas, Monet and Whistler.* Stockholm: Almquist and Wiskell. Atlantic Highlands, N. J.: Humanities Press, 1981.

DURET, Théodore. *Histoire des peintres impressionnistes.* Paris, 1906. *Manet and the French Impressionists.* Tr. by J. Flitch. New York, 1971.

ELDER, Marc. *A Giverny, chez Claude Monet.* Paris: Bernheim-Jeune, 1924.

FELS, Florent. *Claude Monet.* Paris: Gallimard, 1925, 1927.

FELS, Marthe. *La Vie de Claude Monet.* Paris: Gallimard, 1929.

FORGE, A. *et al. Monet at Giverny.* London, 1975.

FOSCA, F. *Claude Monet.* Paris: L'Artisan du Livre, 1927.

FULLER, William H. *Claude Monet.* New York: Gillis Bros., 1891. *Claude Monet and His Paintings.* New York: J. J. Little, 1899.

GEFFROY, Gustave. *Claude Monet, sa vie, son temps, son œuvre.* Paris: Crès, 1922. Reissued and edited by C. Judrin. Paris: Macula, 1980.

GILLET, Louis. *Trois variations sur Claude Monet.* Paris: Plon, 1927.

GORDON, Robert. *Monet.* New York: Abrams, 1983.

GRAPPE, Georges. *Claude Monet.* Paris: Librairie Prestige International, 1909.

GRAPPE, Georges. *Monet.* Paris: Plon, 1944.

GWYN, Stephen. *Claude Monet and His Garden: The Story of an Artist's Paradise.* London, New York, 1934.

HAMILTON, G. H. *Claude Monet's Paintings of the Rouen Cathedral.* London: Oxford University Press, 1960.

HOSCHEDÉ, Jean-Pierre. *Claude Monet, ce mal connu. Intimité familiale d'un demi-siècle à Giverny de 1883 à 1926.* Geneva: Pierre Cailler, 1960.

HOUSE, John. *Aspects of the Work of Claude Monet c. 1877-1887.* London: MA Report, Courtauld Institute of Art, 1969.

HOUSE, John. *Monet.* New York: Dutton. Oxford: Phaidon, 1977.

ISAACSON, Joel. *Monet: Le Déjeuner sur l'herbe.* London: Allen Lane, Penguin, 1972.

ISAACSON, Joel. *Monet: Observation and Reflection.* New York: Dutton. Oxford: Phaidon, 1978.

JOYES, Claire. *Monet at Giverny.* London: Mathews Miller Dunbar, 1975.

KELLER, Horst. *Ein Garten wird Malerei. Monets Jahre in Giverny.* Cologne: Dumont, 1982.

LATHOM, Lady. *Claude Monet.* London, 1931. New York, 1932.

LÉGER, Charles. *Claude Monet.* Paris: Crès, 1930, 1950.

LEVÈQUE, Jean-Jacques. *Monet.* Paris: Siloe, 1980.

LEVINE, Steven Zalman. *Monet and His Critics.* New York, London: Garland, 1976.

LINDON, R. *Etretat, son histoire, ses légendes.* Paris, 1963.

MALINGUE, Maurice. *Claude Monet.* Monaco: Les Documents d'art, 1943.

MAUCLAIR, Camille. *Claude Monet.* Paris: Rieder, 1924. London, 1927.

MOUNT, Charles Merrill. *Monet, a Biography.* New York: Simon and Shuster, 1966.

NOCHLIN, L. *Realism and Tradition in Art 1848-1900.* Englewood Cliffs, N. J., 1966.

PETRIE, Brian. *Claude Monet, the first of the Impressionists.* New York: Dutton. Oxford: Phaidon, 1979.

REUTERAWARD, Oscar. *Monet.* Stockholm: Bonniers, 1948.

REWALD, John. *The History of Impressionism.* 4th ed. New York: Museum of Modern Art, 1980. *Histoire de l'Impressionnisme.* Paris, 1955.

REWALD, John *et al. Aspects of Monet.* A Symposium on the artist's time and life. New York: Abrams, 1984.

ROGER-MARX, Claude. *Monet.* Lausanne, 1949.

ROSSI BORTOLATTO, Luigina. *L'Oeuvre complète de Claude Monet.* Rev. ed. Paris: Flammarion, 1981.

ROSTRUP, H. *Claude Monet et ses tableaux dans les collections danoises.* Copenhagen: Société de l'art français, 1941.

ROUART, Denis. *Claude Monet.* Geneva: Skira, 1958.

ROUART, Denis, REY, Jean-Dominique and MAILLARD, R. *Monet: Nymphéas ou les miroirs du temps.* Paris: Hazan, 1972.

SAPEGO, Igor Gavrilovich. *Claude Monet.* Leningrad: Aurora, 1969.

SEIBERLING, Grace. *Monet's Series.* Doctoral dissertation, Yale University, 1976. New York, London: Garland, 1981.

SEITZ, William Chapin. *Claude Monet.* New York: Abrams, 1960. *Claude Monet. Seasons and Moments.* New York: Museum of Modern Art, 1960.

STOKES, Adrian. *Monet, 1840-1926.* London, 1958.

TUCKER, Paul Hayes. *Monet at Argenteuil.* New Haven, London: Yale University Press, 1982.

VAN DER KEMP, G. *Une Visite à Giverny.* Paris, 1980.

WEEKES. C. *The Invincible Monet.* New York: Appleton-Century-Crofs, 1960.

WERTH, Léon. *Claude Monet,* Paris: Crès, 1928.

WILDENSTEIN, Daniel. *Monet: Impressions.* Lausanne, 1967.

WILDENSTEIN, Daniel. *Claude Monet: Biographie et Catalogue raisonné.* 3 vols. Lausanne, Paris: Bibliothèque des arts, 1974-1979.

We wish to thank the owners of the pictures reproduced herein, as well as those collectors who did not want to have their name mentioned. Our special thanks to the Galerie Schmit in Paris, the Acquavella Galleries in New York, and Los Angeles County Museum of Art for their help.

MUSEUMS

AUSTRIA

Kunsthistorisches Museum, Neue Galerie, Vienna.

FRANCE

Musée d'Unterlinden, Colmar - Musée Eugène Boudin, Honfleur - Musée Marmottan, Paris - Musée d'Orsay, Paris Musée des Beaux-Arts, Rouen.

GERMANY

Staatliche Museen, Berlin - Städelsches Kunstinstitut, Frankfurt - Bayerische Staatsgalerie, Munich.

THE NETHERLANDS

Rijksmuseum Kröller-Müller, Otterlo.

SWITZERLAND

Musée d'Art et d'Histoire, Neuchâtel.

UNITED KINGDOM

National Museum of Wales, Cardiff - The National Gallery, London.

UNITED STATES OF AMERICA

Museum of Fine Arts, Boston - The Fogg Art Museum, Cambridge, Massachusetts - The Art Institute, Chicago - The Cleveland Museum of Art - Denver Art Museum, Colorado - The Metropolitan Museum of Art, New York - Allen Memorial Art Museum, Oberlin, Ohio - Museum of Art, Carnegie Institute, Pittsburgh, Pennsylvania - The Shelburne Museum, Shelburne, Vermont - National Gallery of Art, Washington, D.C. - Sterling and Francine Clark Institute, Williamstown, Massachusetts.

PRIVATE COLLECTION

Mr. and Mrs. A. N. Pritzker.

PHOTOGRAPHS

O. Zimmermann, Colmar - Jörg P. Anders, Berlin - Otto E. Nelson, New York - Lauros Giraudon, Paris - Georges Routhier, Studio Lourmel, Paris - Service de Documentation Photographique de la Réunion des Musées Nationaux, Paris - Artothek, Planegg (Munich).

ILLUSTRATIONS